My family is...

FAMTASTIC

OUR MEMORY BOOK

HERE'S HOW THIS BOOK WORKS:

1. THIS IS MEANT TO BE A MEMORY BOOK FOR YOUR WHOLE FAMILY. EVERYONE IS THE AUTHOR!

2. GO IN ORDER PAGE BY PAGE, OR FLIP THROUGH AND FILL OUT IN ANY ORDER. YOU DECIDE!

3. YOU CAN DATE THE PAGES, SAVE SOME FOR LATER IN THE YEAR, OR FILL OUT THE WHOLE BOOK ALL AT ONCE.

4. FEEL FREE TO MAKE YOUR ENTRIES SERIOUS, SILLY, HEARTFELT, OR FUNNY— JUST BE YOURSELVES!

5. ABOVE ALL ELSE... HAVE FUN!

THIS BOOK HAS BEEN FILLED
OUT BY THE ABSOLUTE BEST,
MOST AMAZING, COMPLETELY
FUN AND ZANY, HANDS DOWN
COOLEST FAMILY
IN THE WORLD. THIS BOOK
HAS BEEN FILLED OUT BY

_____

_____

_____ .

THIS YEAR,

WE ATE

AND DRANK

A LOT!
PROBABLY BECAUSE

.

REMEMBER WHEN

_____

SAID

_____

AND EVERYONE

_____ ?

THIS WAS WILD!

SLEEPS IN THE MOST!

GETS UP THE EARLIEST!

EATS THE MOST, AND

IS THE PICKIEST EATER BY FAR!

A PRETTY *COOL*
HEIRLOOM
WE HAVE IS

_____ ;

IT WAS PASSED
DOWN FROM

.
_____

Out of all of our memories from this whole year, this one has got to be the most memorable of all:

_____ PARTICIPATED IN
_____ THIS YEAR.
THEY *LEARNED* _____
_____.
THEY *LOVED* _____
AND *HATED* _____!

OUT OF OUR EXTENDED FAMILY MEMBERS,

_____

HAS THE WACKIEST TATTOO,

_____

HAS THE MOST OUTLANDISH HAIR,

_____

WEARS THE QUIRKIEST CLOTHES, AND

_____

IS JUST THE ABSURDEST ALL AROUND!

_____ ,

(PARENT)

GROWING UP, WHAT WERE YOUR
FAVORITE PETS
AND WHAT MADE THEM SO SPECIAL?
WHAT WERE THEIR NAMES?

_____

_____

_____

_____

WHILE ON *VACATION*, _____ IS THE PERSON WHO ALWAYS GETS UP FIRST TO GET EVERYONE GOING, AND WE ALL HAVE TO DRAG _____ OUT OF BED BY THEIR FEET.

SPEAKING OF FAMILY VACATION, THIS ONE WAS OUR FAVORITE:

....

....

....

....

....

....

SOME PEOPLE HAVE
FAMILY MEMBERS THAT
KEEP CLOSE *SECRETS.*
BUT WE FOUND OUT THAT
_____'S *SECRET* IS

_____
_____ !

THE OLDEST RELATIVE THAT

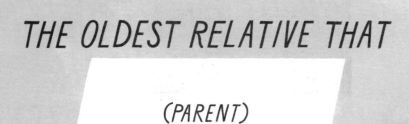

(PARENT)

REMEMBERS IS

.

THIS IS WHAT THEY REMEMBER
ABOUT HIM/HER:

WE'VE BEEN THROUGH
A LOT THIS YEAR.
IT SEEMED THAT JUST
WHEN EVERYTHING
WAS GOING *RIGHT*,
THIS HAPPENED:

AND THEN, WHEN EVERYTHING SEEMED TO BE GOING SUPER WRONG, THIS HAPPENED:

.... HAS THE MOST EMBARRASSING STORY IN OUR FAMILY. I DON'T THINK WE'VE LAUGHED AS HARD AS WE DID WHEN

....

....!

OUR ABSOLUTE FAVORITE MOVIE TO WATCH TOGETHER AS A FAMILY IS

_____ .

AND

_____

IS OUR FAVORITE TREAT TO EAT WHILE WE WATCH.

THE BERMUDA TRIANGLE

AWARD GOES TO

FOR HAVING THE BEDROOM WHERE EVERYTHING SEEMS TO GO MISSING.

REALLY EXCELLED IN

THIS YEAR. I MEAN,
THINK ABOUT IT.
BEFORE THIS YEAR,

HAD NO IDEA HOW TO

.

TIME CAPSULE QUESTIONS! PRETEND YOU'RE GOING TO READ THIS AGAIN 20 YEARS FROM NOW...

(ALL OF YOUR NAMES + AGES)

(TODAY'S DATE)

THE ACTIVITY THAT MADE US LAUGH
THE MOST THIS PAST YEAR IS THIS:

....

INSIDE VOICES? NO WAY! WE WERE
LOUDEST WHEN THIS HAPPENED:

....

WE FOUND THE BEST PLACE TO EAT!

....

IF WE COULD DO ONE THING
AGAIN FROM THIS PAST YEAR,
IT WOULD BE THIS:

....

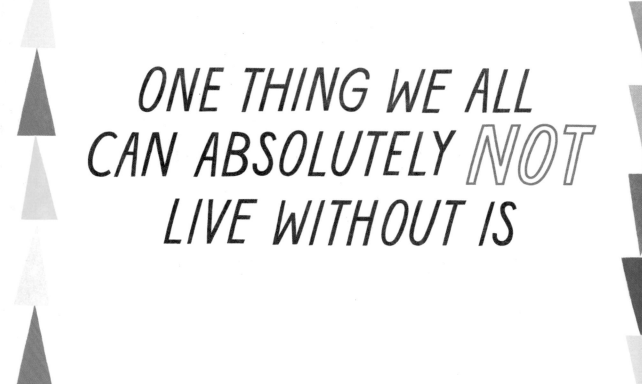

ONE THING WE ALL CAN ABSOLUTELY *NOT* LIVE WITHOUT IS

_____ •

WE MAY NOT KNOW EVERYTHING ABOUT OUR FAMILY HISTORY, BUT WE DO KNOW THIS STORY/FACT:

.....................'S COOKING
CAN BE A LITTLE SCARY,
.....................'S COOKING
IS SIMPLY DIVINE, AND
.....................'S COOKING...
WHO ARE WE KIDDING??
.....................NEVER COOKS!

WHEN THINGS GET HARD
AND WE ALL HAVE TO
STICK TOGETHER,
THE GREATEST THING
ABOUT OUR FAMILY IS

--- .

OUR FAVORITE
SUMMER
ACTIVITY
THIS YEAR WAS

OUR FAVORITE
THING TO DO THIS
WINTER WAS

SPRING
WAS THE BEST
TIME FOR

FALL WAS
PERFECT FOR

WE ALL PRETTY MUCH
AGREE THAT EVERYONE LOOKS
PRETTY RIDICULOUS DOING

_____ ,

PRETTY AWKWARD DOING

_____ ,

AND PRETTY FREAKING
AMAZING DOING

_____ .

ONE OF OUR MOST *FAVORITE* FAMILY MEALS IS

_____ .

HERE'S THE RECIPE:

WHAT ADVICE WOULD WE HAVE GIVEN OURSELVES 1 YEAR AGO?

IF OUR LIFE THIS PAST YEAR
WERE TURNED INTO A FILM,
WHAT GENRE WOULD IT BE?

WHO WOULD BE THE
MAIN CHARACTER?

HOW LONG WOULD IT BE?

COME TO A CONSENSUS TOGETHER!

IS CEREAL SOUP?
WHY OR WHY NOT?

WHAT IS INVISIBLE THAT WE
WISH PEOPLE COULD SEE?

IS A HOT DOG A SANDWICH?
WHY OR WHY NOT?

THE *STRANGEST* THING THAT HAPPENED TO US THIS PAST YEAR THAT MADE US FEEL ALL SORTS OF

WAS

------------------------------------.

*T*HE ETERNALLY LATE AWARD
GOES TO ....
FOR ALWAYS FINDING CREATIVE
NEW THINGS TO BLAME YOUR
TARDINESS ON, SUCH AS A TRAIN,
GETTING CAUGHT IN A PARADE,
THAT THERE WAS A ....
IN THE ROAD, OR ....
.... !

I DON'T THINK IT'S EVEN POSSIBLE TO FORGET THIS *ICONIC MOMENT* FROM THIS YEAR:

OUR *BIGGEST* DISAPPOINTMENT THIS PAST YEAR WAS PROBABLY WHEN

_____.

BUT OUR *BIGGEST* SATISFACTION WAS WHEN

_____.

REMEMBER WHEN

_____

CAME TO OUR HOUSE?
THEY WERE MOST DEFINITELY
THE STRANGEST GUEST
WE'VE EVER HAD BECAUSE

_____ !

WE COULDN'T BE
PROUDER
OF _____
FOR THE WAY
THEY HANDLED

_____

_____ .

IN FACT, WE'RE ALL PRETTY PROUD OF
OURSELVES FOR THINGS WE'VE DONE
THIS PAST YEAR! HERE ARE SOME PRETTY
AWESOME THINGS EACH OF US DID:

_____

_____

_____

_____

_____

_____

IF OUR FAMILY WERE *ARRESTED* AND NOBODY KNEW WHY, EVERYONE WOULD PROBABLY ASSUME WE WERE TAKEN IN *BECAUSE*

· ·

· ·

· .

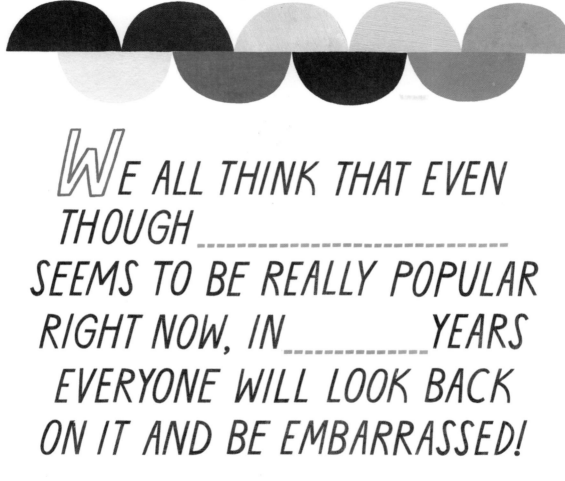

WE ALL THINK THAT EVEN THOUGH _____ SEEMS TO BE REALLY POPULAR RIGHT NOW, IN _____ YEARS EVERYONE WILL LOOK BACK ON IT AND BE EMBARRASSED!

WHAT DID WE *WORRY* ABOUT THIS PAST YEAR THAT WE PROBABLY SHOULDN'T HAVE?

WHAT WAS ONE THING WE PROBABLY SHOULD HAVE TAKEN MORE *SERIOUSLY*?

OUR ANCESTORS FROM

··

WOULD BE PROUD OF US
TODAY BECAUSE WE CARRY
ON THE TRADITION OF

··

··

IF WE WERE ALL TRANSPORTED
500 YEARS INTO THE PAST
TO LIVE, WE'D BASICALLY KICK
BUTT AT _____.
WE WOULDN'T _____
SO WELL BECAUSE _____
_____.
AND WE ALL AGREE THAT
WE'D NEED TO LEARN HOW TO
_____ QUICKLY!

IF WE HAVE TO LISTEN TO _____ COMPLAIN

ONE MORE TIME

ABOUT _____,
WE ALL MIGHT START
PULLING OUR HAIR OUT!

THIS PAST YEAR, THE MOST EMBARRASSING THING WE ALL DID TOGETHER WAS

--- .

THIS WAS _____ !

AND _____ !

REMEMBER WHEN THE CRAP HIT THE FAN AND

....

.... HAPPENED?
TALK ABOUT CHAOS!

SOME OF OUR *UNIQUE* FAMILY TRAITS INCLUDE

_____, _____,

AND _____.

_____ IS OUR FAVORITE!

THE DUCT TAPE
AWARD GOES TO

_____

FOR BEING ABLE TO FIX
JUST ABOUT ANYTHING
AND EVERYTHING!

COME TO A CONSENSUS TOGETHER!

HOW MANY CHICKENS WOULD IT TAKE TO KILL AN ELEPHANT?

WHAT'S THE ABSOLUTE WORST NAME SOMEONE COULD GIVE THEIR CHILD?

IF PEANUT BUTTER WASN'T CALLED PEANUT BUTTER, WHAT WOULD IT BE CALLED?

AN *OBSTACLE* THAT
WE FACED TOGETHER AS
A FAMILY THIS YEAR WAS

_____ .

WE OVERCAME IT BY

_____

_____ .

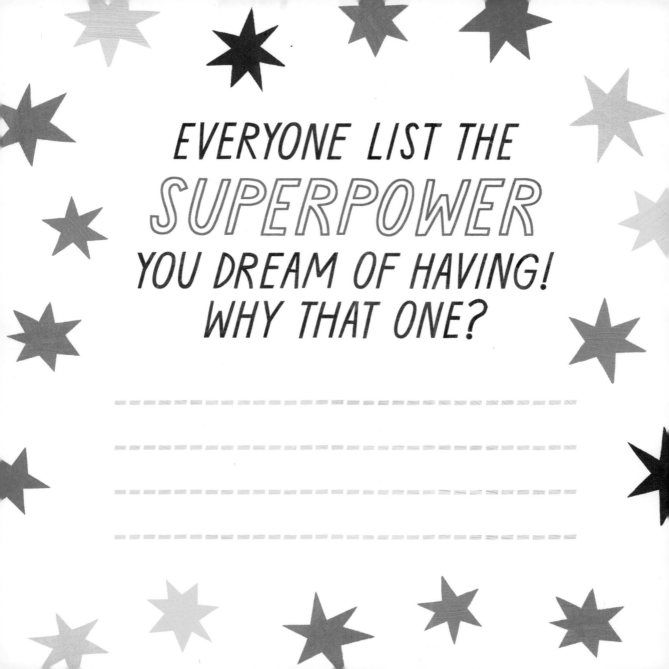

EVERYONE LIST THE
SUPERPOWER
YOU DREAM OF HAVING!
WHY THAT ONE?

EVERYONE LIST 3 WORDS TO DESCRIBE THE PERSON SITTING TO YOUR LEFT!

....

....

....

....

....

IF WE GOT 3 WISHES
TO MAKE FOR NEXT YEAR,
THEY WOULD BE THESE:

EVERYONE ALWAYS SAYS,
"NO REGRETS!"
BUT WE ABSOLUTELY
REGRET THIS MOMENT:

_____

_____

_____

THIS EXTENDED FAMILY MEMBER ALWAYS HAS THE *BEST STORIES* TO TELL. OUR FAVORITE IS THIS ONE:

HERE ARE SOME THINGS WE KNOW ABOUT ....:

(ANY EXTENDED FAMILY MEMBER)

BORN IN:

RELIGION:

EDUCATION:

PROFESSION:

GREATEST ATTRIBUTE:

When the world seems topsy-turvy, and everything is backward and not forward and upside down instead of upside right...

_____ IS THE BEST AT MAKING US COME TOGETHER AND LAUGH.

_____ IS THE BEST AT MAKING SURE WE FEEL SAFE AND LOVED.

_____ IS THE BEST AT

_____.

AND WE'RE ALL PRETTY GOOD AT

_____.

OUR FAMILY
ORIGINATED FROM

,

AND WE CAN TRACE OUR
FAMILY LINE BACK TO

.

WE WOULD ALL
BEST DESCRIBE OUR
HERITAGE AS

_____

AND

_____ .

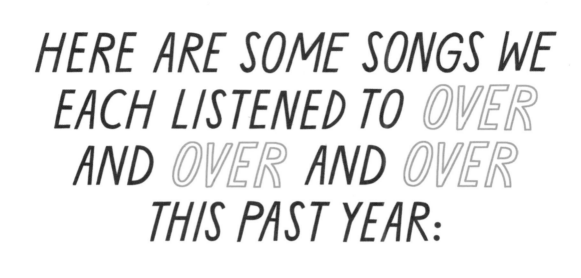

HERE ARE SOME SONGS WE EACH LISTENED TO *OVER* AND *OVER* AND *OVER* THIS PAST YEAR:

• •

• •

• •

• •

SPEAKING OF SONGS,
IF WE ALL HEAR

_____

ONE MORE TIME, I THINK WE'LL
ALL SMASH THE RADIO!
WE MAY EVEN

_____ !

IN A ZOMBIE APOCALYPSE, _____ WOULD DEFINITELY BE THE FIRST TO DIE. _____ WOULD SCARE AWAY THE ZOMBIES JUST WITH THEIR _____ ALONE...

_____ WOULD WHISPER TOO LOUDLY AND KILL US ALL, AND _____ WOULD STICK THEIR HEAD IN THE SAND AND PRETEND THEY WERE IN TAHITI.

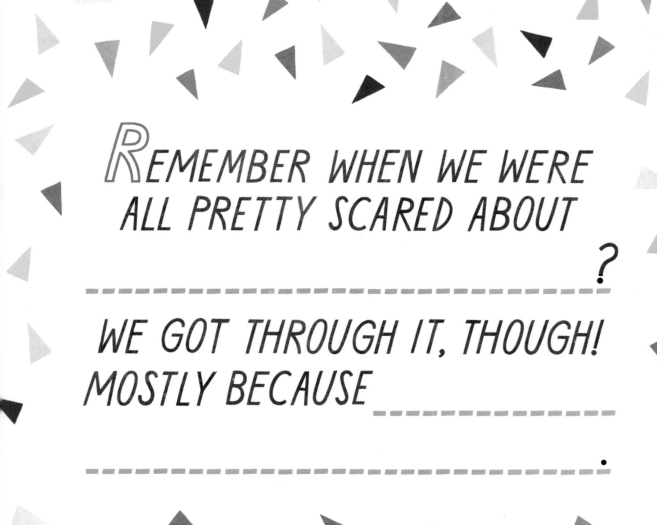

REMEMBER WHEN WE WERE ALL PRETTY SCARED ABOUT

_____ ?

WE GOT THROUGH IT, THOUGH! MOSTLY BECAUSE _____

_____ .

THE *BEST GIFT* WE RECEIVED THIS YEAR WAS

_____ .

AND THE *BEST GIFT* THAT COULDN'T BE WRAPPED IN A BOX OR PUT UNDER A TREE WAS

_____ .

THERE ARE SO MANY THINGS
TO BE GRATEFUL FOR, LIKE
MAYBE CHOCOLATE-COVERED

_____

OR EVEN _____ .

BUT MOST OF ALL,
WE'RE PRETTY GRATEFUL FOR

_____ .

WE WOULD ALL PROBABLY *FAINT* IF WE MET

-- --

BECAUSE -- -- -- -- -- -- -- -- -- -- -- -- -- -- --

-- --

IF WE COULD ALL BE FLIES ON THE WALL, WE WOULD WANT TO LISTEN IN ON

....

BECAUSE ....

....

WHAT CAN BE FOUND AT AREA 51? WE DON'T KNOW FOR SURE, OF COURSE! BUT HERE'S WHAT EACH OF US THINK MIGHT BE THERE:

_____

_____

_____

_____

_____

_____

THE MOST REWARDING ACT OF KINDNESS WE ALL DID THIS PAST YEAR WAS _____ BECAUSE _____

_____

_____ .

LET'S CHOOSE AN ACT OF KINDNESS TO DO TOGETHER NEXT YEAR! EVERYONE COME UP WITH ONE OPTION, WRITE IT ON A STRIP OF PAPER, DUMP THEM IN A HAT, AND CHOOSE SOMEONE TO DRAW ONE STRIP. THE WINNING ACT OF KINDNESS IS

!

IF WE COULD SUM UP THE
PAST YEAR TOGETHER IN
ONE WORD EACH,
WHAT WOULD OUR WORDS BE?

THE BEST KIND OF MEMORIES ARE MADE TOGETHER. AND IF WE HAD TO CHOOSE JUST ONE MEMORY THAT WE WOULD REMEMBER FOR THE REST OF TIME, WE'D CHOOSE THIS ONE:

------------------------------------ .

GIBBS SMITH
TO ENRICH AND INSPIRE HUMANKIND

25 24 23 22 21   5 4 3 2 1

Written by Kenzie Lynne, © 2021 Gibbs Smith

Illustrated by Melanie Mikecz, © 2021 Melanie Mikecz

Published by
Gibbs Smith
P.O. Box 667
Layton, Utah 84041

1.800.835.4993 orders
www.gibbs-smith.com

Designed by Melanie Mikecz

Printed and bound in China
Gibbs Smith books are printed on either recycled, 100% post-consumer waste, FSC-certified papers or on paper produced from sustainable PEFC-certified forest/controlled wood source. Learn more at www.pefc.org.

ISBN: 978-1-4236-5820-7